Nurture

Being

ADAM BULBULIA

Nurture Being

Published by

HEART-CENTERED
REVOLUTIONS

ISBN: 979-8-9860416-0-5

Dedication

This book is dedicated to the teachings of Lao Tzu. Without him I would have been lost for so many years wandering through the wilderness of identifying with my separate sense of self. Lao Tzu, thank you for sharing your wisdom with us, and Stephen Mitchell, thank you for your most beautiful translation of Lao Tzu's words. Of all the translations I've read, it feels like you penetrated the essence of the words and brought them into the English language, so I didn't need to master Chinese to understand these profound teachings. I also want to thank nature, herself, for everything. She has taught me this most sacred and profound art to nurture the very depths of Being. Human nature has been one of the greatest mysteries to me. Thank you, Being, for the mystery and joy of existence.

CONTENTS

Introduction

We are human beings. It's right there in our name what we are. Beings! And yet who truly understands the nature of being? When we nurture being we become a living embodiment of the feminine principles of life nurturing the whole of our existence. We all come from the mother. Literally, we are born from our mother's womb. And our existence is sustained by the great forces of the feminine. This book is meant to be a model for how to come into a deeper relationship with your being through the kind act of nurturing being. The more you nurture being, the more you become deeply connected to your being in every sacred moment of life.

How to Use this Little Book

This book is meant to be a living experience not just words in a book, or on the computer or phone. I've included 30 second experiences that are designed to help you take the content more deeply into your life. You may take up to five to ten minutes with any of these experiences if you want to feel them more fully. However, they are designed to be effective in a short 30 second mini experience.

With the 30 second experiences, read each step slowly, and embody the experience briefly before moving on to the next step. Take the time to let the exercises touch your heart. They are meant to remind you of who you really are underneath all the layers of conditioning. Know that any of the experience are not for you unless they resonate for you.

When you return to living from your deeper being, everything in life flows more easily. Enjoy your journey with this book, the rest of your life, and beyond. May this book serve you and help you grow into who you truly are. Creating this book has been a powerful journey for me and I hope it serves to nurture your whole being.

Nurture Being

Self-care is essential to everything. Wherever we go in life the self is the one constant. When we take care of our 'self' everything in our life flows better. The most profound act of self-care possible is to nurture being. When you nurture your being, all your actions come from a place of deeper connection and love.

Nurturing being is born out of the art of being. This is an art of allowing. It is unfolding your leadership by letting the potential inside of you emerge. This potential comes forth naturally when we allow ourselves to be ourselves. We do not try with our thinking capacities to make ourselves different from how we naturally are. Instead, we let ourselves be. Nurturing stems from the feminine principle of sustaining and allowing something through our loving attention.

When we nurture being, we become role models to others around us by the simple act of being ourselves. When we are simply being, we are leaders. Being is the most profound act we can ever embody. It is not what we say that matters here; it's who we are.

1

Being is Allowing

Allowing is the opposite of control. We allow outcomes to unfold, we don't manipulate them. In fact, when we are truly practicing this, we don't control what we say or do. We allow our actions and our words to flow through us from deep inside. The right action makes itself apparent through us when we surrender and let life flow like a river. It's like being in the zone where the dance emerges effortlessly as we let go and allow.

In Being we live and let live. We don't try to control anything or anyone. We don't control our own actions. We allow ourselves to be as we were meant to be, and we allow others to be as they are meant to be. When others are inauthentic, it's okay to point that out. In fact, it's the most loving thing you can do for another. Society calls it rude, but our being loves honesty. We allow being and support being. Allowing is accepting. Allowing is letting go. Allowing is the essence of wisdom. Allowing is brave. Allowing is heart opening. Allow life to happen through you.

Experience: *Allowing*

Purpose: To allow and surrender to events in your everyday life.

Use this when: You are resisting life, struggling, or just want more flow. Use this every day.

1. Find something in your life that you are trying to force. It could be the timing of an event, a relationship dynamic, or anything that you are pushing to make happen.

2. Take a deep breath, and let go of trying to force it.

3. Open to allowing it to unfold effortlessly. It's like grasping something with your hand and then letting it go.

4. Feel how it feels to let go, and simply allow it to be, as it is.

5. Rest in this allowing for as long as you like.

6. When you return to acting in the world, continue allowing.

7. Allow, throughout your day, and notice what changes.

2

Being is Listening

Being is Listening. When we are being, we listen to the forces of nature. We listen to the wind as it rustles the leaves. We listen to the birds singing their sweet songs. We listen to all the other beings, we feel, and we open to what is. Listening brings us almost as close to our being's core as feeling. When we listen we open to the music of life all around us. Listening is sacred and sweet. When we listen we can hear the magic of the universe.

We can listen when we are alone and we can listen when we are with others. We can listen when others are speaking and we can listen when we are speaking. There's no limit to the amount of listening possible as we deepen our presence in being. Listen, listen well. Expand your listening. Listen to everything.

Experience: *Listen, Listen, Listen*

Purpose: To listen to everything in your surroundings and inside of you.

Use this when: You're not tuned-in, or you want to enhance your sense of your environment. Practice listening every day in every possible way.

1. Listen! Notice all the sounds you hear around you.

2. Feel, as you listen, and let the sounds move your heart.

3. Listen to what is happening inside of you.

4. Notice the sounds of your body, mind, and heart.

5. You are the listener. As you listen, let yourself be.

6. Continue to deepen your listening as you come back from the exercise.

7. As you move through your day, listen to everyone from this deeper space of being.

3

Being is Feeling

Being includes both feeling and thinking. The core of being is more directly experienced through feeling than through thinking. When we truly feel, we are opening to a new experience of what is occurring right now. Feeling is an act of sensing the unknown. Emotions are known labels to sensations that we've worked out in our minds. Feelings are the raw sensations themselves. When we feel, we step out into the dark and open to it. We welcome the newness of it. When we open to feelings, we open up to an ever deepening journey to the center of being.

Feelings are facts of inner perception like what we see with our eyes. Feelings are what we feel with our heart and body. Feelings help us discover possibilities that we have yet to dream of. All feelings can be felt, experienced, and loved. When we love all our feelings, our presence in being naturally deepens. As our presence in being deepens, our capacity to feel opens. We naturally embody our fullest potential when we feel.

Experience: *Open to Feeling*

Purpose: To open to feeling and center in your heart.

Use this when: You're out of touch with feeling or want to connect more deeply to your feelings. Use this often and repeatedly whenever you can. Feel every day in every possible way.

1. Place your hand on your heart as you open your awareness to feelings.

2. Notice how you feel at this moment.

3. Let it be a completely new experience. It's like feeling an inner wind, washing through your insides as it breathes new life into you.

4. Relax and allow more feeling to come forward as you spend the remainder of the time allowing yourself to feel what you feel.

5. Simply notice, allow, feel. Notice, allow, and feel anything that arises inside you.

6. As you return from the exercise, keep noticing, allowing, and feeling what you feel. As you carry on with your day, gently return to this place of feeling whenever you remember. Feel, open, allow.

4

Being Centers in the Open Heart

When we are being, our heart naturally opens. And when our heart opens, we are naturally being. It's actually very simple. Be yourself and your heart opens to life. Try to be different and your heart closes. When you allow yourself to be, just as you are, just as Nature, God, or the Universe meant for you to be, everything opens up for you.

One's true being loves all – it does not discriminate. Our being feels a deep love for humanity and loves all life. Our true being naturally loves all other beings. When we feel this love from the deepest recess of our being, we know we are swimming in a vast ocean of unconditional love. And when we are identified with being, we are both the ocean and the swimmer. We cannot tell the air apart from our own body. We are at one with all that is.

The heart is the center of your being, and opening your heart to love centers everything inside you. When you center yourself in your heart everything flows from being. Every action you do, every thought that you have, every experience you experience, can be centered in your heart. When you live with your heart at the center, your life becomes a living prayer of unfolding love for all of humanity.

Experience 1: *Center in your Heart*

Purpose: Center your Being in your heart for balance.

Use this when: You are feeling off center, out of alignment with your heart, or wanting to center more deeply. Use this process daily or several times a day. It is the very center of your being and will put you in touch with everything else you need and want.

1. Lay your hand on your heart and allow your heart to open. This is your center.

2. Feel the love for your being. Admire the beauty and radiance of who you truly are.

3. You are beyond the sun, moon, and stars. Your being is radiant beyond Venus's light. You are amazing!

4. Feel the unconditional love in your heart for your being. This love will always be here to center you in your heart.

5. Send this love out to all beings. You can imagine any specific being you want to feel this love, and just let it radiate from your open heart. You can also imagine it radiating out like a star to all beings.

6. Appreciate the pure being of your loving heart. This is your center, your core, and your essence.

7. Make your heart the center of your existence. When you lose touch with your heart, throughout the day, return here. Touch your heart as often as you need to and remember this is your home, your center, and your core. You are heart-centered!

Experience 2: *Open the Heart of Love*

Purpose: To center your being in unconditional love.

Use this when: You're needing more access to love. This process will help when you're feeling alone, disconnected, or just stuck in general.

1. Place your hand on your heart and allow your heart to open. This is your center, your home, and your essence.

2.   Breathe deeply and notice how it feels as you let yourself feel your heart even more.

3.   Feel into the inner core of the heart and notice the softness here.

4.   Feel the pulse of your heartbeat that is keeping you alive.

5.   Love everything about your heart and thank it for keeping you alive.

6.   As you return to the flow of life, touch your heart periodically, and remember this sustaining force that is underneath everything.

7.   Keep loving your heart as you move through your day. Know that your heart is the center of your life.

5

Being is Open Minded

The Being has no fixed ideas or prejudice. The Being welcomes all thoughts and doesn't discriminate against them. The Being can discern with the heart which thoughts serve life and which thoughts don't. The Being gravitates to what serves the whole and steers away from what fosters division. When your mind is as open as the sky, thoughts can come and go as they do without disturbing the still, deep waters of your being. Any thought that comes through is allowed in the pristine beauty of your open mind. Welcome them all and let them go. There is no need to attach to them. They are advisors from the beyond. And they come and go as they please when we let them flow.

Experience: *Open the Mind*

Purpose: To let go of attachment to beliefs and fixed thoughts. To free your mind from the shackles of conditioning.

Use this when: You're in a mental rut, or stuck in a habitual way of thinking. Or any time you want to open your mind.

1. Take some core fixed idea you have about a person or life itself. You'll know it is a fixed idea because it limits you in some way, it pigeon holes you, another person, or life itself.

2. Ask yourself is this really true?

3. Experiment by letting the thought go and letting yourself settle back into the unknown.

4. Feel the emptiness in your mind of not knowing and not attaching to any thought.

5. Let go of all thinking itself and settle back into being. Letting go doesn't mean you stop thinking - it means you stop identifying with your thoughts and simply allow the process to happen.

6. Breathe and be as you are.

7. Open your mind and expand to the limitless possibilities here.

8. Thoughts come and go as your mind opens to the flow of thinking. Thoughts are beautiful, welcome them, and let them go.

9. Feel your being grow as your mind opens, by allowing the flow of thoughts to be as they are inside the mind. Letting yourself think as you naturally think, without any conscious interference, is one of the most relaxing and peaceful experiences.

10. Enjoy the peace of allowing the openness of your mind to be like the sky, welcoming all into its embrace.

6

Being Honors the Body

Our being manifests in the body in this lifetime on earth. Being doesn't push the body or ride the body like an uncaring person riding a horse. Being understands that without our body there is no life on earth. Being embraces every little ache and pain. Being honors the body's experience.

When you love your body, only then can you truly be at ease with yourself in this life. When you are at war with your body you are at war with yourself and life. Love your body with every action you take. Be good to your body, take care of your *self*, and nurture this sacred temple that houses your heart, soul, mind, spirit, and being. Being has nothing but gratitude for the great mystery of body. There is a lifelong love affair the Being has with the body. Even when you are single you get to have this amazing love affair.

Experience: *Love Your Body*

Purpose: To love and appreciate every part of your body and connect more with the fullness of life.

Use this when: You want to feel love for every and any part of your body. Use this often to center yourself and balance your energy.

1. Center in your heart, the core of your being.

2. Feel the love you have for life here.

3. Turn your attention toward your body. Shower your body with love.

4. Start with your head and bring love to your eyes, nose, ears, hair, brain, jaw, cheeks, lips, tongue, mouth, and face. Love every part of your head. Smile at it and rejoice as you love each part.

5. Bring this loving attention down to your neck, shoulders, elbows, biceps, triceps and forearms. Love your wrists and your whole hands right to the tips of your fingers, and fingernails. Let each area relax as your loving awareness touches it.

6. Embrace your heart and chest, lungs, stomach, small intestine, large intestine, liver, kidney, pancreas, and adrenals.

7. Love each vertebrae of your spinal cord moving from top to bottom. Love your

whole back, upper, middle, and lower back. Bring your loving attention to your hips.

8. Love your genitals and reproductive organs.

9. Love your thighs, knees, hamstrings, calves, ankles, and feet.

10. Love every part that was missed between the fingers, toes, and tips of your hair.

11. Love your skin as this most sacred container of your physical body.

12. Love any part that calls to you. Love any part that wants more attention or honoring.

13. As you move through your day love your body in every action and celebrate this life-long love affair between your being and your body.

7

Being Inspires Joy

Being is a joyous experience. Being is a celebration of all that is. Life flows through us like water through a stream. Being is joy. It is like a child in their natural state of play.

Being is all we need to return to our fullness. Simply being is all we can do. It's so relaxing. It's so easy. It's so joyous. Remember your being. Embrace your joy. Play every day in every possible way. Remember what it was like to be a child and feel the thrill of living. Dance, play, and be the being of joy you were meant to be.

Experience: *Experience Joy*

Purpose: To connect with the joy of being.

Use this when: You're out of touch with the joy of being and want to deepen it. Use it often and enjoy it.

1. Place your awareness inside for a moment and notice you're alive. Your heartbeat is one of the most vital signs of life. Feel it as you notice you are alive.

2. Think of the last thing you experienced that
    was joyous. It might be watching a sunrise, or
    seeing someone you love smile, petting your
    dog or cat, eating a food you enjoy, or the
    touch of your lover's hand.

3. As you remember this experience, feel the
    simple joy in being.

4. Bring this joy into the present moment as
    you notice yourself here and now.

5. Be grateful for getting to be here on earth
    having this experience right now.

6. Be grateful for the joy. Open your heart and
    let yourself feel it fully.

7. You can say, "Thank you for the thrill of
    being alive."

8. Say, "Thank you life for bringing me so
    much joy!"

9. As you move through your day, play with this
    joy. Do little fun games as you move
    thorough space that make your life more
    enjoyable. Remember that this life is meant
    to be a joyous adventure.

10. With all the seriousness and heaviness in the world, we honor this and we still play like children in the face of the tragedy of existence on earth at this time. We dance and enjoy life while feeling the grief and weight of human existence. Joy is our birthright. We claim it without denying anything. We are beings of joy.

8

Being is Simple

Like the heart, the being is simple. Life is a flow of love – it simply flows through us. It is the easiest, most natural thing in the world to be. Being in the flow of love it is easy to surrender. Yet many of us have rarely experienced this. When we become mature enough all we want is to be. Our heart naturally opens to our being. We simply allow love and truth to unfold. We are Being. Life is simple.

Experience: *Find Simplicity*

Purpose: Experience the simple nature of Being.

Use this when: You feel overwhelmed or want to connect with simplicity. Practice this every day or anytime you want.

1. Notice what you are thinking about and simply stop tracking the flow of thinking.

2. When we stop focusing on the thinking, our being emerges.

3. Feel the simplicity when your thoughts stop hooking your attention and your being comes forth.

4. Being is a relaxed awareness that opens to the moment.

5. Open to simply being yourself right now.

6. There's nothing you have to do. Just be as you are.

7. As you breathe in and out, allow, and be.

8. Smile. And simply allow yourself to be at peace. This peace naturally washes over you with the simplicity of letting yourself be.

9

Being is Natural

Being is simply being true to our nature. There's nothing you need to learn except to unlearn what is not in your nature. It's like taking off your clothes to experience your essential naked nature. You were born naked. You were born being. It's the most natural thing imaginable. Natural is simply doing what you feel moved to do and not judging or filtering yourself in any way. Being natural is allowing what is inside your nature to come out without any conditions on it. Being is the most natural thing in the world.

Experience: *Experience your Natural Being*

Purpose: Experience the naturalness that is core to your human nature.

Use this when: You feel far from yourself or want to return to your very essence.

1. Take off any stress like you take off your shirt as you enter a bath.

2. Strip away any pretense and be naked before life.

3. Be honest with yourself about how you are right now. How do you really feel?

4. This is your natural state. Right here, right now.

5. Allow yourself to be right here, as you are, in this present moment.

6. You can say to yourself, "Ah, my natural being."

7. Take your time being here until you want to return to being in the flow of your daily life.

8. Keep being natural as you return to whatever you do next.

9. Simply let yourself be as you are and do what you feel moved to do.

10

Being is Easy

Being has a kind of ease and grace to it. Being is easy. It takes no effort, just relaxation. And yet, we all need practice remembering how effortless and easy it can be. It's like letting go of the stress from your jaw or your head. There are ways in which we hold tension in our body without knowing it.

If you've ever received a massage, you know the experience of suddenly realizing how tense you were, but only after you stopped carrying the tension. The more tension we hold in our body the less we are able to feel. Simply tense your bicep or whole arm and hold it. Notice how you can feel the tension. Now let it go. In the relaxation in your arm you can feel the whole arm, not just the stress. Stress limits our focus. Ease expands our focus and allows us to be. Relax and be at ease.

Experience: *Practice Ease*

Purpose: Experience the ease of being.

Use this when: You want to bring ease into every action that you do. Use this whenever you are putting too much effort into something.

1. Take any action and do it with ease.

2. Pick up your phone, or another object nearby, and do it slowly and with ease. Do it as if it were the easiest thing in the world.

3. Now bring that ease into your next action.

4. Notice where there's tension in your body and relax that tension while feeling even more ease as you do it.

5. Life is meant to be easy. Enjoy it!

6. Let yourself be and flow with ease.

7. Bring this ease into the rest of your day. And remember, whatever you do can be done with more relaxation and ease.

11

Being is Grateful

There is so much in this life to be grateful for. In being we are grateful for our parents. We are grateful for all those we have learned from and we are grateful for all the difficult experiences that brought us to where we are now. Being is an act of gratitude. We know without all our relations we are nothing. And in every step, every breath, and every word we have gratitude for nature, our ancestors, God or the Universe, and for life itself.

Experience: *Embody Gratitude*

Purpose: To adopt the right attitude to promote being.

Use this when: You want to connect with gratitude. Use this frequently to return to the focus on being grateful.

1. Touch your heart, and feel your awareness center here. Be grateful for your heart that's giving you life.

2. Turn your attention to all the people, animals, and plants that have assisted you in this life. Feel your gratitude for them.

3. Notice your ancestors and your lineage. Without your parents, and their parents, and so on, you couldn't be here in this body. Feel the way your life rests on their lives. Extend the gratitude in your heart to all your ancestors.

4. As you breathe, be grateful for the air around you. Without it you have no life. As you walk, notice the earth under your feet supporting you. Thank the earth for giving you a home here.

5. Remember all the water that flows in your blood. Be grateful that we still have enough water to drink.

6. Be grateful that we still have a loving sun shining on us. The stars and planets, moon, and the great sky above are here for us everyday blessing our existence.

7. Turn your attention to your friends and all your family. Feel gratitude toward all of them or any of them in specific.

8. Just open your heart with gratitude and shower the love in the direction of your choosing.

9. Feel gratitude for the forces that are behind life itself. God, the Universe, the Force or whatever name you want to call it by. Feel gratitude for all that sustains life and nurtures it with love.

12

Fear Blocks the Flow of Being

When we live from fear we limit the potential for being. Fear tells us we're wrong. Fear pulls us into the future with worry. When we embrace fear and respond authentically, it's all okay. Fear is no obstacle for an open heart. Fear shows us our edge. Any time we move to our edge we feel fear. Fear is not a problem; fear is a teacher. Acting unconsciously from fear is the root of all evil. Embracing fear allows you to dispel evil or unconsciousness anytime you want.

Experience: *Embrace Fear*

Purpose: To free yourself from living in fear.

Use this when: You are feeling the presence of fear bearing down on you. Use it anytime you want to embrace your fear more fully. Use this often to find the hidden fear.

1. Notice where you are feeling fear.

2. Instead of pushing it away, welcome this fear energy.

3. Invite the energy and allow yourself to be with the energy.

4. Love the sensations and energy you've been labeling as fear, just as it is. What does it feel like? Is it hard or soft, sharp or dull, tight or loose, moving or still?

5. As you notice how it feels, nothing needs to change.

6. Embrace everything you feel. Embrace the sensations and energy fully.

7. Notice how the energy of fear changes when it is accepted. Feel how good it feels when you accept your fear.

8. This is your lifeforce and vitality. Enjoy it!

13

Being is Courageous

It's strange to say this, but being ourselves in this culture is an act of courage. Every animal and plant does this effortlessly and it's no big deal for them. For a human being in these times, it takes profound courage to be ourselves. The path that is laid out for us is one that has us following the bad advice of others or the diseased dominant culture itself. The sickness of our culture will consume all life if things don't change.

It is time that we learn to go our own way in true collaboration with others. It's time to go the way of the heart. Courage is the way of the heart. Courage comes from the French word 'coeur' which means heart. When we embrace courage we speak the truth. It does not matter whether or not the truth is popular. We take a stand for what is right, good, and true and plant our flag here.

Experience: *Find Courage*

Purpose: To transform any obstacle into fuel for courage.

Use this when: You are experiencing a challenge, obstacle, or anytime you want to experience more courage.

1. Sense an obstacle that's holding you back from being authentic. (Such as a person, a belief in your head, some fear, a general sense of pressure to be a certain way that does not serve you.)

2. Turn and face this obstacle, and simply be with it and breathe. Don't try to fix it, just allow it to be here.

3. As you look directly at this issue, notice your courage in facing this. Honor and celebrate your courage. Follow your heart now and let go of the pressure to be different than how you actually are.

4. Take the path of courage. Listen to it and trust it to lead you to your destiny.

5. Thank the original issue for helping you to face yourself more fully.

6. Touch your heart and honor it for its ability to feel, face, and live life. It's not always easy but you are here. You are alive.

7. Your courageous heart allows you to face life

14

Being is What We are Meant to Be

We are human beings. Could we possibly be anything other than who we are? We are meant to be who we truly are. Yet many of us are not being ourselves. We are lost trying to be how we think we're supposed to be or how someone else is. When we simply be as we are, we become a force that serves all beings.

Be a model to the world and surrender to who you really are. You get to be yourself. There's no one in the world that could possibly be better at being you than you! You came into this life with a specific mission and purpose. And you get to fulfill it by being yourself.

Experience: *Be Yourself*

Purpose: To be as you were meant to be.

Use this when: You're feeling pressure to be different.

1. Notice where you are feeling pressure to be a certain way. (At work, in a relationship, or with your family, etc.)

2. Stop listening to the voices of the pressure.

3. Simply let them go, and allow yourself to be as you are.

4. Who you are is what you were born to be. Don't try to change it.

5. Just let it be and relax.

6. You get to be yourself.

7. It's the only true job you ever get to have. It's the only thing you can truly do. Enjoy it.

15

Being Helps Fulfill Our Destiny

When we simply be as we are, it's as if we enter the fast track to fulfilling our destiny. By following the innate instructions on the inside, it sets us on a clear path to live life to its fullest. Trying only gets in the way. When we are trying to regulate how we are, or trying to be someone else, we delay our destiny. And yet, even trying is a part of our unfolding path. The best way to find who we are is to discover who we are not. This way we can discern our authentic self from inauthenticity.

The instructions for how to deal with every moment of life are embedded in the very fabric of our being. There's no right way to approach any situation. And there's a way that's true to our nature to approach any particular situation. When we let ourselves feel and notice what is authentic to us, our natural response emerges. When we honor our natural response we activate the built in code to unlock our full potential and fulfill our destiny one step at a time. This code is written in our heart.

Experience: *Fulfill Your Destiny*

Purpose: To pair your breathing and walking with fulfilling your destiny.

Use this when: You are breathing or walking and want to be more connected with your destiny. Use it always or whenever you want.

1. Touch your heart, open it, and allow yourself to be.

2. What if each step you take is a fulfillment of your deepest destiny. Walk as if each step brings you closer to the fulfillment of your destiny.

3. Let the unfolding of your destiny grow naturally like a fruit ripens or a flower blossoms.

4. Notice a recent difficulty you had in the last day or week.

5. Just breathe and be and notice you are closer to yourself from going through the difficulty.

6. With each outbreath, let go of anything in the way of your destiny. With each inbreath, breathe in the energy you need to face your

destiny. Every breath brings you closer and closer to your heart's desire.

7. This is your destiny awakening from the inside. Feel it. Open to it. Love it. And welcome it.

8. Place this exercise in the background of your awareness as you breathe, walk, and move through your day. Any time you want to do it more consciously, bring it back to the foreground. This way you can keep it going without conscious attention.

16

Being is Letting Go

When we let go and open to our deeper being, we don't need to control or force things. Being allows us to go deeper. Being allows us to observe the natural order of things. When we are being, we open to the underlying rightness in all things. Like a fruit ripens, in time, our being knows there is no rush to get anywhere. The ego roots for outcomes much the same way that a sports fan desperately wants their team to win. And there's no problem with rooting for outcomes or teams. It's just when the ego gets locked in the pursuit of outcomes, we lose sight of what we are here to learn and unfold through each experience. We can allow the process to unfold naturally and effortlessly.

We all want what we want. And life gives us a combination of what we want and what we don't want. When we completely embrace what we don't think we want, then we can truly let go. We can allow and let go of any need to control outcomes. Whatever comes, we know we can learn and grow from it. We can be open. We can let go.

Experience: *Let Go*

Purpose: To let go of attachment to beliefs and free your mind.

Use this when: You feel you are efforting, your ego is clinging to something, or you feel constricted.

1. Take your ideas about yourself like how good or bad you are at something, how successful or messed up you are, or any identities that you believe define you, (parent, profession, or any underlying characteristic like hobbies or behaviors you do) and let them go.

2. Breathe out, and simply let them all go out of your body. Breathe in life force, and breathe out and let go of who you think you are.

3. Let go of any attachment to a particular outcome you've been invested in.

4. Allow yourself to be as you are, without trying to control or grasp anything.

5. Breathe and continue to let go of all thoughts.

6. Let your feelings wash over you, allow, and let go.

7. Simply allow yourself to be, and let go of anything in your way.

8. Keep letting go and allowing with every breath you take.

17

Being Precedes Becoming

Being comes before becoming. Like a sunrise, everything in nature happens through being. In a sense, being is more important than becoming. When we focus on being, we naturally become. When we focus on becoming, it leads to trying to be different from how we are. When we focus on being, everything unfolds from here. All the forces of nature operate from being and not from trying. The way a flower blooms, the way a seed sprouts, the way a tree spreads roots, are all acts of being.

Experience: *Find Being Underneath*

Purpose: To connect more deeply with your being.

Use this when: You feel disconnected or stressed while doing.

1. Take an action you recently performed.

2. Go back in time to just before you went into motion.

3. Notice the state of being that preceded the
    action.

4. Dwell in this state of being, and enjoy the
    peacefulness here for the remaining time you
    focus on this exercise.

5. Notice there are layers of being underneath
    where you are.

6. Drop into a deeper layer of your being by
    simply shifting your focus, and let yourself
    feel more and open more deeply.

7. As you come out of this exercise, keep
    feeling the deeper place in your body, where
    your actions are arising from now.

8. This state is a deeper layer of being, and it's
    underneath everything you do.

9. Feel your being underneath, and relax into it.

18

Create Environments to Nurture Being

We can create a culture that supports being in our friendships and in our work relationships. When we make our work culture support each person in being themselves, we have a revolutionary company. When we make a friendship or romantic relationship where the other gets to be all of themselves, then we have a revolutionary friendship, or romantic relationship.

Most of human society functions around control and fear. We are afraid of our nature, so we create rules to try to control ourselves and each other. If we truly trusted each other, we wouldn't need rules. We would live and let live. We would love and trust in the goodness inherent in all things.

Experience: *Create a Nurturing Inner Environment*

Purpose: To create an inner environment that is suitable for self-love and growth.

Use this when: You feel negativity or bad feelings toward yourself, or when you want more love for yourself.

1. Notice any place, in your body, that feels judgmental towards self.

2. Let go of any judgments. Seeing that they are untrue, since they are judgments, just release them from your mind with an out breath.

3. Breathe out judgment, and breathe in acceptance and love.

4. Let your whole state of being emerge, and let it surround you with acceptance and love for who you are.

5. Allow all your feelings to be, just as they are.

6. Notice how it feels to be in an environment that fully supports and loves you.

7. Let the love into your heart.

19

Unconditional Love Fosters Being

Unconditional love creates the environment that fosters and nurtures being. We all thrive in an environment where we are loved, unconditionally, just as we are. When we surround ourselves with people who are supportive and loving, it is so much easier to realize our dreams and fulfill our potential, in contrast to when we're with unsupportive or judgmental people.

Experience 1: *Love Unconditionally With an Easy Person*

Purpose: To deepen your unconditional love with someone you easily already like.

Use this when: You want to take your unconditional love deeper with someone you already like. This practice will also help deepen unconditional love in you.

1. Direct your attention to someone else who is easy to love. It can be a person, animal, plant, star, or anyone.

2. Shower your person, animal, star, or plant with unconditional love. Radiate energy from your heart warmly and freely as if it is a shining sun.

3. Love them for being them, without any desire for them to change or be different. Simply appreciate and love them as they are.

4. Now extend your focus to include yourself. Let the same level of love flow unconditionally to you. Nothing needs to be changed. Just love yourself as you are.

5. Notice how self and other merge in unconditional love. Just let the love wash over all that you are as you love both yourself and the other.

6. As you return to yourself, feel the new found love in your heart.

7. Continue tuning into the love as you feel moved throughout the day.

Experience 2: *Love Unconditionally With a Challenging Person*

Purpose: To deepen or develop your empathy and unconditional love with someone who is not easy for you to love.

Use this when: You're challenged by someone and you want to open your heart and love them more. Anytime you want to have deeper empathy with a difficult person, this practice will assist you.

1. Direct your attention to someone who is challenging for you to love (a difficult person, a former lover, an enemy, or anyone who is hard for you to love).

2. Open to all the feelings you have about this person.

3. Let yourself completely accept and love all your feelings about this challenging person. (You may need some time here before moving on. If that's the case, you may want to stay at this step for as long as it takes before moving on. Love the feelings you have about them in the background of your awareness until you are ready. Continue with the next steps in a day, a week, or whenever you feel ready.)

4. When you have complete acceptance for your feelings about the other person, put yourself in the other person's shoes. Notice their place of wounding that has made it

difficult for them. Notice in what ways they may be coming from fear or a challenging circumstance.

5. Now love this person for being themselves without any desire for them to change or be different.

6. Appreciate the difficult role they've been playing in your life. They've taught you a lot through their unconsciousness and your own unconsciousness around them.

7. Forgive them and yourself, as you allow them to simply be as they are, and you as you are.

8. Notice how good it feels as you forgive, accept, and love them just as they are.

20

Being Unfolds with the Seasons

Everything in life has seasons, cycles, and patterns. When we understand the seasons, we can stay at the center of things, and not attempt to force anything. There's a time for being alone, and time for being together. There's a time for taking outward action, and a time for having inner reflection. There's a time to create, a time to preserve, and a time to destroy. There's a time to live fully, and a time to surrender to death. All things have their seasons. Allow your Being to unfold with the seasons.

When you follow the natural impulse of your being, you don't have to tamper with things or meddle in outcomes, unless you want to. The true way will unfold before you, as ground emerges under your feet when you walk. Trust that you will be held. There's nothing to fear. The Being knows no fear. The only fear we experience is from being caught in our separate sense of self. When our ego is in brave service to our being, our ego knows how to face fear so it can stay dedicated to our deeper being.

Experience: *Surrender to the Seasons*

Purpose: To connect more deeply with the seasons of life which are underneath every experience.

Use this when: You're having difficulty accepting a situation. This practice helps you embrace the impermanence in all things and know that everything changes like the seasons. Use this frequently to fully embrace the changes in your life.

1. Notice something in your life that's challenging. It could be a situation around a person you're in conflict with or a state of being (like being single, without a job, or without a home).

2. Remember that this is happening just for a season.

3. At some point this state or experience will pass into another state or experience. It will not always feel this way. It will not always be this way.

4. Embrace all that you feel around this particular season you are in. Let yourself feel

in your body all the resistance and fear you experience. Simply allow it.

5. Honor this season as it. This will pass. Enjoy the experience you're having while it lasts, even if it is difficult. One day you may miss this experience like an old friend. Even though it has been challenging, notice the rightness in this experience. Life couldn't have reached you any other way.

6. Savor every little bit of the experience like a tasty morsel of your favorite food.

7. Extend your gratitude to this experience as your most excellent teacher.

8. Honor and love the season you're in. One day it will flow into the next season much like winter flows into spring or summer into fall.

9. Allow the seasons to be as they are. Let go. Embrace. Love.

21

Lead from Being

The very best leaders are tapped into a source of Being underneath everything. They lead from their being in the service of all beings. When we bow down at the altar of being, and serve human potential in every interaction, then we are truly honoring our being.

Experience: *Lead from Being*

Purpose: To ground your leadership and all your actions in being.

Use this when: You are practicing leadership in any way.

1. Before you lead another, make sure you are connected to the source.

2. Feel this connection to your deepest being, the way a tree sends its roots deep into the earth.

3. Ground yourself in your deepest being and let all your actions flow from here.

4. Touch your heart and notice it is the center of your being.

5. Thank your heart for being so strong and sustaining your life.

6. Go forth into the world and act with your heart leading you.

22

Being Doesn't Seek Approval

Being is not concerned with approval. Being honors the depth in all things and does not seek surface measures of success. When we become beholden to another's approval, we become their prisoner. When we honor that we are as we are, we need no external validation. Appreciation and outward approval is good when it happens, but we don't seek it out.

Experience: *Un-attaching from Approval*

Purpose: To realize that your being needs no approval from anyone.

Use this when: You feel overly invested in what someone else thinks of you, or wish to untangle from any person you feel too close to in an unhealthy way.

1. Think about the person's opinion that you value the most, or a person you feel you are in some way trying to please.

2. Let go of any attachment to being any particular way for them, just as you let go of air from your lungs as you breathe out.

3. As you breathe in, rest in the fact that who you are is beyond any need for approval.

4. Just breathe out, and let go of trying to please. And breathe in deeper self-acceptance.

5. Keep letting go of any need for approval on the outbreath, and inhale deeper self-acceptance on the inbreath.

6. You can continue this practice for the rest of your life just by pairing the outbreath to letting go, and the inbreath to taking in acceptance.

Note: As you continue this practice simply let it run in the background of your awareness, and shift the focus of the exercise to whichever person you're trying to please at the time. Anytime the practice needs your attention, you can focus on it again in the foreground. Profound changes happen if you keep this intention flowing over the course of a week. You'll naturally be less and less concerned about pleasing others.

23

Being is Comfortable in the Unknown

Being doesn't need to work everything out ahead of time in the mind. Being knows there is a natural order in things, which is beyond calculation, and trusts in the rightness of how things unfold. Being embraces the unknown mystery.

Experience: *Embrace the Unknown*

Purpose: To embrace the unknown dark mystery that life is.

Use this when: You feel uncertain or uncomfortable about the unknown.

1. Take something that you are struggling to understand.

2. Let go of any desire to know or grasp it in your mind.

3. Simply allow it to be, as it is, with all the great mystery surrounding it.

4. Breathe out, and let go of control or trying to understand. Breathe in, and embrace the great mystery.

5. Continue to let go and embrace as you breathe.

6. Feel into how you feel about this.

7. Let all the feelings wash over you as you continue to breathe, allow, and embrace. Continue breathing, allowing, and embracing for as long as you live.

24

Being Doesn't Seek Perfection

Being knows it is not perfect and is perfectly itself. Being doesn't seek to be better, prized, remembered, or famous. Being is how it is and allows events to take their course. By not striving, the being rests in the present moment. Knowing there is nothing to achieve, all struggles evaporate. Feeling the inherent goodness underneath we can let go of trying, and simply be.

Experience: *Let Go of Trying*

Purpose: To experience the flow of life from a more surrendered place of being.

Use this when: You are feeling like you are putting too much effort toward something and want to be in a more surrendered state.

1. Notice an area where you are trying to be better or improve yourself too much. You'll know it's too much, because you feel some stress around this tendency.

2. Breathe out, and let go of any trying whatsoever.

3. Notice when you breathe out and let go fully, the inbreath naturally comes without any effort.

4. Trust in your natural response. No effort is needed to force anything.

5. Surrender to the perfection you truly are by simply being yourself.

6. As you move through your day, notice yourself trying and putting extra effort into things. Let go and be at ease as much as you want in your daily doing.

25

Being is Born Out of the Unseen

Emptiness is brimming over with so much potential. What already exists is formed. What doesn't yet exist is what we use to shape outcomes and move toward potential. The unseen forces, which support life, give birth to all beings. Much like the 'force' in the Star Wars movie series, there are unseen forces behind life. These forces are physically represented by the sun, moon, stars, and planets.

Experience: *Connect with the Unseen Forces*

Purpose: To cultivate a deeper connection with the unseen forces that support life.

Use this when: You are disconnected or wanting to feel more connected with all that is.

1. Notice there are forces all around you working for your best interest.

2. Feel these forces of love and light supporting you like the stars and the sun support you even when you don't see them.

3. Feel, allow, and embrace all the support from the unseen forces. Let them guide your life.

4. Next time you see the stars wish upon them as a child would, and draw on the power of their light and love.

5. Love them the way they love you.

6. Honor the forces behind the stars and love them the way they also love you.

7. Be grateful for all the unseen forces that are assisting you.

26

Being Doesn't Chase Outcomes

Being is content with things as they are unfolding. It's as okay with failure, as it is with success. Being understands that we learn more from our setbacks and welcomes them with equanimity. It doesn't rush or strive to get somewhere. It allows the unfolding to unfold.

Experience 1: *Let Go of Outcome*

Purpose: To be more open to being by letting go of outcomes.

Use this when: You feel attached to an outcome and want to let go.

1. Notice something that you desperately want to happen.

2. Feel the desire for it, embrace the energy of the desire, and let go of being attached to the outcome.

3. Just breathe into it until you let go of any desire to control or push for what you want.

4. Let yourself want what you want, without the energy of making it happen.

5. Allow the events surrounding this desire to unfold naturally.

6. Feel the relaxation as you become fully present right now.

Below is a second practice to help you let go of outcomes. This practice takes the wind out of the sails of a difficult experience. Oftentimes, we manifest difficult experiences to help us feel the feelings we have not wanted to feel. This practice helps us give up our attachment to things going well, which, ironically, makes it more likely for things to go well!

Experience 2: *Embrace the Worst Possible Outcome*

Purpose: To imagine the worst possible outcome so you can open up possibilities.

Use this when: You are afraid or avoiding something that you do not want to have happen.

1. Notice something that you really do **not** want to happen.

2. Imagine the worst case scenario happening.

3. Feel all the feelings you would have if it happens in the worst possible way.

4. Locate where you feel the feeling specifically, in your body.

5. Accept all the feelings you have here. If there are any judgments against those feelings, allow them to release as you embrace these feelings.

6. Know that you are resilient. You can handle anything. Know that even the worst case scenario can never truly stand in your way.

7. You are unstoppable!

27

Being Fosters Wholeness

Being aware of the whole is an essential facet of being. When we are being truly ourselves we look out for the whole. When we lose touch with being we become self-absorbed. This self-absorption takes us out of being. From the perspective of being, we love this self-absorption and it is no problem for us. It is just a state we cycle through sometimes. Even evil, in this sense, is just a momentary imbalance seeking to return to the light of wholeness.

Experience: *Be Wholeness*

Purpose: To get in touch with the underlying wholeness of a situation and embody it more fully.

Use this when: You feel like you need the whole picture on something. Or to be able to sense the wholeness in a situation or a dynamic. Use this all the time every day.

1. Take something that is happening and feel the whole field of the situation.

2. Include yourself in the field as a necessary part of it all, along with everyone else.

3. Ask yourself, "What is best for this whole field?"

4. Do that and see what happens next.

5. Keep holding the whole field of any situation throughout the day.

6. Love the ones you are with and rejoice in the wholeness of it all.

28

Being is Beyond Gender

The Being is neither male nor female; it is both, and beyond. It is neither cisgender nor transgender; it is both, as well as beyond. The being is not bound by gender conditioning. Gender conditioning and gender identity are core parts of the personality and need to be honored. Being embraces all gender identities without any discrimination. When we let go of identification, this is only for the purpose of feeling the expanse of who we truly are at the deeper layers of being.

We are not trying to change any gender identification. We are not saying that it's how you should permanently identify at the deeper layers of being. We are simply allowing the fullness of our being to blossom through letting go of attachment to some core feature of personal identity. Gender identity is a controversial and multifaceted issue. If you don't resonate with this approach at this time, it is not for you. Move on to something you resonate with, either inside this book or elsewhere.

Experience: *Let Go of Gender Identification*

Purpose: To experience Being beyond any notion of gender.

Use this when: Just once, so you have an experience of it. And you may return to this practice any time you feel trapped in gender conditioning.

1. Notice the gender you identify with. Notice the conditioning that comes with this gender identity.

2. Breathe out, and let go of any thoughts about yourself related to gender.

3. Breathe in, and know that the Being has no gender and has all genders.

4. Swim in the infinite vastness of your Being beyond any polarity or definition.

5. Notice the freedom beyond any ideas of gender.

6. Simply be as you are without regard to any rules or ideas of what and how you are supposed to be.

29

Being is Beyond Race

The personality exists within both racial and gender constructs. Race is defined by the mind and thus it is a social construct not an inherent principle of existence. Racial identity is a core part of how many of us identify in our personal sense of self. Being knows no skin color and does not distinguish people by their genitalia nor gender identities.

Taking on a shift in identity may be difficult if you have experienced strong discrimination for your race or skin color. Often discrimination leads us to identify more deeply with whatever features are being discriminated against. Know that it is okay if this practice does not resonate for you. Take what you need from all the words here, and just leave the rest behind.

Racial identity is a huge problem in our culture. This exercise does not address the social and political issues associated with race. It is only meant to help you deepen your personal relationship with your being. Know that this practice, or any of the practices, are not for you unless they resonate for you.

The being sees only the qualities of heart and soul each person possesses. This open perception can be misconstrued as not honoring culture. Being honors all diversity of culture, race, gender, and sexuality. Because it is beyond them all and includes them all, Being can embrace and fully love them all.

Experience: *Identify Beyond Race*

Purpose: To experience being beyond any notion of race or skin color.

Use this when: Once, simply to have an experience of it or any time you feel trapped in racial conditioning.

1. Notice what race you identify with or skin color you have. Notice all the stories that come with this racial identity.

2. Let go of the identification with race and all the attached stories.

3. Just breathe out, and let any ideas based on race gently leave your body. Breathe in the fullness of being, allowing yourself to feel who you are as a human being beyond any sense of race or skin color.

4. Experience yourself as a Being of pure consciousness and sentience beyond any forms or labels.

5. Open to the Being that is beyond race and settle into this experience.

6. Notice how you feel as you let go of this core feature of personal identity.

7. Embrace the expanse of being beyond race.

30

Being is Beyond Sexual Orientation

However you may identify: as straight, gay, or
bisexual, pansexual, asexual, or any of the myriad
ways to identify, Being is beyond all of them.
Sexual orientation is core to our personality, and
it is very important to us at this level. Letting
sexual orientation go does not mean you change
anything about how you identify or who you are
attracted to. In fact, your sexual orientation will be
right here waiting for you at the end of the
exercise, just as your gender identity and racial
identity are. You just don't need to hold onto
them so tightly. These identities can be held at the
personality level, like your preference for your
favorite hobby or activity. At the being level you
embrace all hobbies and activities as perfectly
valid. You still get to like what you like at the
personality level.

Experience: *Let Go of Attachment to Sexual
Orientation*

Purpose: To experience being, beyond any
notion of sexual identification.

Use this when: Once, simply to have an experience of it or any time you feel trapped in conditioning around sexual identification.

1. Notice how you sexually identify.

2. Notice all the ideas that come with your sexual identity and who you are attracted to.

3. Settle into your deeper being and let go of believing your sexual identity is core to your being.

4. Breathe out and let go of any ideas or notions of who you are attracted to.

5. Breathe in and allow yourself to notice who you are beyond any sexual preference.

6. You simply are as you are.

7. You simply love the ones you love.

8. Feel the freedom of being beyond any sexual identification.

9. You contain sexual identification and attraction. You are not limited by it.

31

Being is Beyond Diagnosis

Being is not autistic, nor neurotypical, or it is both and neither. This is another core aspect of personality that our true being is beyond. Being honors autism just as it honors neurotypicality. Whatever pathways your brain moves in, or however you experience the world, Being embraces all pathways. Having any diagnosis, such as depression, bipolar disorder, addiction, narcissistic personality disorder, ADD/ADHD, schizophrenia, or other medical condition, does not define our being. Our Being is beyond any particular way of thinking or identifying. Diagnoses have their place, and can be extremely helpful for understanding ourselves, and any definition is confining to the Being.

Experience: *Being Beyond Labels*

Purpose: To experience Being beyond any notion of diagnosis and labels.

Use this when: Once, simply to have an experience yourself beyond diagnosis or neuro labels.

1. Notice whether you identify as autistic or neurotypical (non-autistic) or both.

2. Notice any conditioning about any other diagnosis you may have.

3. Let go of any need to label your neuro pathways or any other aspect of your being through the lens of diagnosis.

4. Allow yourself to be as you are and notice how you think without any restriction from a specific label.

5. Let your experience of life be what it is.

6. Let go of any labels you have around how your brain functions. All diagnoses – ADD/ADHD, depression, anxiety – need to be let go of in the light of being.

7. Simply allow yourself to be without any mental baggage clouding you. Let your light of being shine through the clear window of your completely open mind.

32

Being Doesn't Compete

Being wants all beings at their best and does not compete. Being enjoys competition as a child does, but has no investment in winning or any outcome of the game. Being loves the game itself. Enjoy all games and play, knowing as the Being all you seek is to enjoy, evolve, love, and learn.

Experience: *Transmute Jealousy into Inspiration*

Purpose: Shift any jealousy to desire.

Use this when: You feel jealous of another person or excessively admiring of them.

1. Notice someone you feel jealous of or admire.

2. Focus on their skills and just lean into the full admiration of these skills in the other person.

3. Know that these gifts, or gifts like them, also reside in you.

4. Let their flowering be an inspiration to you.

5. Feel the inspiration open your heart.

6. Be grateful for their gifts.

7. Let their gifts open up your gifts. Feel the desire for your gifts to blossom. Love the desire and trust in its rightness.

33

Being Lets Events Go Their Own Way

When we are being, we know we don't have control over events and we allow things to flow. We let people go their own way and we let events run their course. We also let ourselves intervene whenever and wherever we feel moved to, as we do not try to control ourselves either. We let all things go the way they want to go.

Experience: *Allow the Natural Unfolding*

Purpose: To let things unfold as they are.

Use this when: You're trying to control what's happening.

1. Notice an event or process that is occurring.

2. Let it unfold exactly as it is unfolding.

3. Let yourself only do the actions you feel moved to do from your being - nothing more and nothing less.

4. There is nothing you have to do and there's nothing you have to not do.

5. Simply allow the thing to unfold and allow yourself to unfold with it.

6. Do whatever you want as it all unfolds.

34

Being Does Not Seek Power Over, It Seeks Power With

As the band Tears for Fears says in their song, "Sowing the Seeds of Love," Being sings: "I believe in love power." This is the only kind of power Being is truly interested in. It has no desire to control or exercise power over others. The Being loves to love and enjoys the power of togetherness that comes with love.

Experience: *Power With*

Purpose: To experience more collaborative power with another.

Use this when: You want more collaboration with another or there is some power dynamic.

1. Feel into a person you want to have power with.

2. Notice how they are, as you feel into them.

3. Ask yourself the question: how can we work more fully together to get what serves both of us here? What is the win-win?

4. Let your intuition guide you to be more deeply tuned in to ways of relating with them.

5. Notice if there are any truths you want to express to this person.

6. When you interact with them, practice what you got from your intuition and find the win-win in each situation wherever and whenever possible.

35

Our Being Shines Like a Star

The star is the best metaphor in physical reality for our being. It is light and radiant in every direction. When we find our true nature we shine like a star beyond any notion of doubt, beyond any limitation.

Experience: *Shine Like a Star*

Purpose: To let the full light of your being shine to the farthest reaches of the universe.

Use this when: You feel small or want to radiate more fully.

1. Let the full radiance of your light permeate all around you.

2. Imagine you are a star giving off light in all directions.

3. Feel what it is like to radiate this light all around you.

4. You are the light of the world.

5. Open your heart and let your original soul shine through.

6. There is nothing small about your being. You have a large mission and purpose and you belong here just as you are.

36

Being Connects Us to Our Origins: Our Original Soul

Being is our home. It is where we come from and where we all return. When you honor the deeper magic in being, you know there is no place to get to and nothing to do. All you need to do is allow yourself to feel the origins of who you are in your heart, soul, spirit, body and mind, and let yourself naturally blossom into who you are. Being connects us with the home inside our heart which can never die even when our physical heart stops beating. Being connects us to the original place of soul where the spark of us originated.

Experience: *Return to Your Origins*

Purpose: To have a larger sense of who we are by connecting to where we come from.

Use this when: You want to return to the origins of where you come from or when you feel ungrounded or purposeless. Use this on a clear night when you can see the stars.

1. Look up at the night sky on a clear night when you can see the stars.

2. Open your heart and deeply feel your connection to it.

3. Breathe, relax, and be, as you feel your heart.

4. As you gaze up at the stars, feel for where you truly come from.

5. Trust your intuition and feel for your origin. Let an image of your true birth place or where you came from before birth arise in your mind's eye.

6. Feel a connection settle into this origin spot.

7. It is your home and the grounds for your being.

8. And this home is right here inside your heart.

9. Notice your feet on the Earth and embrace your home on the Earth for as long as you're here.

37

Honor and Let Go of the Past

The past is to be honored. It got you here. Without it you wouldn't be who you are. Your parents brought you into this world. If you were adopted then you have two sets of parents to be honored. When we honor our parents, no matter how shitty or good they were, we honor our heritage. When we honor our upbringing, and how we came to be here, we honor our Being.

When you are truly present, the story of who you have been is constantly evolving. As you tell the same story over and over about how you came to be who you are, you limit yourself. Letting go of the sense of self found in history can be quite liberating.

Experience 1: *Honor the Past*

Purpose: To free yourself from the hold of the past by honoring it.

Use this when: You feel stuck in the past or when you simply want to have gratitude for anything that came before this.

1. Touch your heart and connect with the love inside it.

2. Turn your loving attention to your birth parents and everyone who raised you.

3. Let yourself feel everything you feel about them. If you have unresolved issues needing attention, stop here and explore and love what you feel until you are ready for the next step. (This could take a moment, an hour, a day, or a week.)

4. Love and honor your birth parents. Thank them in your heart for all they provided for you. Without them you don't have this life.

5. Thank them for the great gift of life. No matter how bad they were to you in certain ways, you would not be here without them. They were your portal into this life.

6. Honor everyone who raised you. Honor all your teachers, friends, family, and everyone who got you to where you are today.

7. Honor all the experiences that shaped you into who you are.

8. Thank all the experiences and people and bow to your great past.

Experience 2: *Let Go of the Past*

Purpose: To find freedom in being, through letting go of the past.

Use this when: You are stuck in the past and you cannot find your way out.

1. With each breath, center deeper in your heart.

2. Notice how you identify with your upbringing or the story of who you have been.

3. Let go of any need to identify with anything that you were.

4. Breathe out who you have been and breathe in who you are right now. Let go of any story about the past that doesn't need to be held in your energy. It is your history and nothing more and nothing less.

5. Open to the moment as you are right now. Being welcomes the past, but is in no way confined or defined by it. Being is eternal and stands outside of time and space.

6. Stand in this place beyond time and admire your life.

38

Being is Immortal

Our bodies will die as will our separate sense of self. Our Being is immortal. Our deepest being was never born and thus it can never die. Our deepest being exists outside of time. We fear death as an end. Yet when we know where we came from we know where we are returning. All life flows back to the source just as all rivers flow toward the ocean. We are not bound by time. Time is bound up inside of our deepest being.

Experience: *Remember Your Soul's Immortality*

Purpose: To reexperience where you came from and where you are going – to remember that you are immortal.

Use this when: You want to have an experience of where you came from, or any time you want a reminder of the spirit world, and to feel your right place in and outside of time.

1. Feel into a time from before you were born.

2. Notice that you were conscious and aware before birth.

3.   Where did you come from? Feel and open to the timeless experience of who you were before this lifetime.

4.   If you want to take more than 30 seconds, feel free to do this as you settle into your origins.

5.   Notice all the images and feeling impressions you have from before this lifetime.

6.   Now imagine your death. Where do you go after you die?

7.   Notice you return back to your birthplace, only changed from your experience here.

8.   You are beyond death and birth. Your being is immortal.

39

Being is Beyond the Stars

In order to fully experience the vastness of our Being, we must look up at the night sky and know that our Being is all that and more. Our whole experience comes from this deeper source of being. It can be called God, the Tao, the Universe, or the Force. However, you know this source, it is beyond our manifested existence. We are limited in perception by our personal sense of self. It is only when we step back from this sense of self that we can truly embrace all that we are.

Experience: *Open Beyond the Stars*

Purpose: To get in touch with the largeness of your being.

Use this when: You are stuck and need a larger perspective.

1. Look at the stars or the sun. If you're looking at the sun, remember all the stars that are behind the sun that you cannot see because the sun is shining.

2. Notice who you are beyond the stars and beyond any notion of the self.

3. Let yourself open to an experience beyond any idea of who you are.

4. Experience the deep reality of your being unfolding here – right now – like a true force of nature.

5. Your being is vast and beyond the universe. Open to it and feel it.

6. Your ego is small and your being is vast.

7. From your vastness embrace the smallness.

40

Being Lets Go of Illusions, and Surrenders to Reality

Take things as they really are. Let go of any illusions, any assumptions, or any judgments in your mind. Let go of any fixed ideas about life itself needing to be a certain way. Let go of it all. Being opens to whatever experience brings. When we have no fixed ideas, we are open to all. You can feel and sense illusions and false beliefs in your heart. When you dwell in your heart you live in reality.

Experience: *Let Go of Illusions*

Purpose: To let go of false beliefs and open your mind.

Use this when: You feel trapped in bad beliefs or limiting thinking.

1. Feel into a current or past situation and notice any beliefs you might have about that situation.

2. Notice which beliefs feel off to you and are therefore false.

3. Knowing that they are false, let them go with the outbreath.

4. Open to the unknown truth of existence without any beliefs.

5. Simply open to what is at the core of everything.

6. Let go of all illusions and open to the truth that stands before you, inside of you.

7. Relax and feel the ease of your being beyond any illusions.

8. Simply notice what is, breathe, and embrace it.

9. This is reality. It is no better or worse than what is. Accept reality as it is.

41

Love the Ego

The ego is not a problem but a necessary aspect of life for human beings. The ego allows us to feel our sense of separateness. Without this sense of separateness so much of the experience of life would be closed off to us. The ego is a psychological skin holding us together. The ego is not a mistake and there is nothing wrong with it. It is when we identify with only our ego that life becomes a problem or series of problems. Deep seeded ego identity is the root of all imbalance in humanity.

When we are suffering or struggling in life, typically it is because we are identifying with our ego. It is part of life to dance between our ego and our being. The good thing is there is a quick and easy fix to being stuck in the ego. It is right here inside yourself at all times. Simply love the ego. When you love the ego you cannot be the ego since you are the ego's lover. Being is the ego's lover.

Experience 1: *Love the Ego*

Purpose: To develop more ability to identify with the Being.

Use this when: You are feeling stuck or identified in the ego.

1. Notice where you feel separate or stuck in a personal ego identity (when you are stuck in a position, feel like a victim, or just acting like a little entitled nincompoop).

2. Feel your heart with your hand and open to your deeper being.

3. Remember this bigger sense of self that the Being is.

4. From this expanded place, love your ego.

5. Embrace every feeling of separateness and isolation it feels.

6. Welcome every little insecurity and fear.

7. Welcome every aspect of the ego as you would embrace a child that you dearly love.

Note: The paradox is this: the best way to not be ego identified is to let yourself be ego identified!

Your mind may trip on this; but experience it out, you will find it is very effective. This next practice is a profound form of *allowing*. When you have no preference on your state of being and allow yourself to be as you are, then there is no resistance to what is and you naturally return to a state of being.

Experience 2: *Identify with Ego*

Purpose: To be ok with identifying with Ego.

Use this when: You want to practice identifying with your ego to develop more ability to be okay with wherever you are.

1. Start wherever you are and let yourself identify with your ego, your personal identity.

2. Touch your heart and let it open deeply to how you are just as you are.

3. Direct your attention toward something you really want to have happen and fully identify with your egoic desire to control and have it your way.

4. Think of possible negative outcomes and let yourself be afraid that you might never get what you want.

5. Experience the sense of separateness and cut-off-ness the ego feels.

6. Notice the places you feel unlovable or unloving.

7. Allow yourself to be here and fully let yourself identify with your ego.

8. It is no problem to be identified with your ego. It is a natural aspect of being human.

9. It's all good, even the shit that's not. Embrace it all!

42

Being is the Answer to the Great Question

As we pursue the ultimate question about what is the meaning of life, the universe, and everything, here we are! We get to make the meaning we find in it. Is there an inherent answer to this question? Search your heart and your being and see what you find.

I find there is an answer that I can never convey to you with words, yet it is here in the rising sun. I notice an answer when I gaze at Venus, Jupiter, Sirius, and Arcturus. It is in the full moon's rise, the ocean's tide, the flow of the river, the still mountain's strength, and the quiet star-filled desert's sky.

It is right here in the eyes of your baby or the touch of your lover's hand. It lives in the wisdom of the tallest and smallest trees of the forest, and it is here in the bird's song which fills our daily skies. It is here in the human heart, and in the presence of love that touches all things great and small. It dances in your fingers and toes and pumps through the blood of your body touching every organ. You might sense it on the tip of your nose, taste it on your tongue, and experience it in all the many pleasures of life. It lives inside the heart of Being in All Things.

Experience: *Design your Own 30 Second Exercise*

Purpose: To practice creating your own exercises and find your own way to truth.

Use this when: Anytime you wish or your when your Being calls you to use it.

1. Come up with steps that most fit for getting at the essence of whatever you desire.

2. Set up five to nine steps for yourself as you open more and more to life.

3. Make your words an inspiration to you.

4. Enjoy every aspect of it. Savor it and feel it open your heart and your being.

Final Point:

Let Go of Any Idea

All fixed ideas about anything limit life, including what I am saying right now. Anything we can say about life or think about life, places a limit on the unlimited potential that we can only point to or suggest with words. Words at their very best are poetic pointers to the deeper truth. When you let it all go, only then can you embrace the fullness of your being. Let go of all conceptions of truth, life, God, and everything. Find what you feel and experience directly with your heart.

Experience: *Let it All Go*

Purpose: To step into true and unbiased experience.

Use this when: Anytime.

1. Breath in the life force of the universe. Breath out all beliefs.

2. Continue breathing, and on the next out breath, let go of your beliefs about religion, God, atheism, or science.

3. Keep breathing, let go of any stories you
    have about yourself, your history, and what is
    possible or impossible.

4. Let go of everything you believe about
    anyone else.

5. Now let go of anything you believe about
    yourself or life itself.

6. Keep breathing. Open now to the truth that
    is beyond any concept or idea.

7. Open to the truth that speaks for itself in
    your being.

8. Feel the truth touch your being deeply and let
    it all go as you embrace your being.

9. Feel it all in your heart. Open your heart and
    let the love of all that is be with you as you
    let go of anything else.

10. Open to the love as fully as you desire.

How to Continue this Work

If you want to speed up your evolution with <u>Nurture Being</u>, there are courses available.

Visit the website at <u>heartcenteredrevolutions.org</u>. You can also follow us on Youtube, Facebook, and Instagram.

We have monthly in-person courses, zoom courses, and self-paced courses. I also offer one-on-one work to take this more deeply into your daily life. I offer sessions individually, with couples, and I offer 15 minute Essential sessions where we get to the core of what is going on to bring resolution quickly to the issue.

Words After Words

Thank you for embarking on this journey together into your being. I hope you feel more of your full being now and forever. May every breath, every step, every sight, every sound, every touch, every thought, every feeling, and every experience bring you closer and closer to the core of your being for as long as you exist. May each action be a play of Being unfolding inside of you. Enjoy the great song and dance that life is. As the famous Navajo prayer says, "It is finished in beauty." Or has it just begun?

Love *Allways*,

Adam Bulbulia

Made in the USA
Middletown, DE
22 July 2022

69744388R00066